Stopping Joseph Kony

Fighting for Peace and Justice in a Viral World

Tim O'Connor
Bannon River Books

Table of Contents

Copyright

Genesis

Viral Media and Social Change

Who is Joseph Kony?

What's been done to Stop Him?

Invisible Children – The Backstory

KONY 2012 – The Movement

Criticisms of Invisible Children and KONY2012

Next?

Endnotes

Copyright

Trust only movement. Life happens at the level of events, not of words. Trust movement. ~Alfred Adler

You should know that, other than personally pledging his support to Invisible Children, the author is not affiliated with Invisible Children, Inc. or the KONY2012 campaign per se.

All references to the organization and the movement are made in good faith. There is no attempt to defame or bring damage to either. All references reflect due diligence in trying to accurately report the back-story and events as they unfold.

Invisible Children, Inc. is a 501(c)3 tax-exempt organization. Any references to the KONY2012 campaign are by nature of reporting on the positive success of the movement and in no way imply the use of any registered trademarks or designs.

First Published, April 1, 2012

Genesis

I came to this project – this e-publication – out of curiosity, concern, and not a little outrage. My curiosity was spurred by the viral nature of the KONY2012 video, my concern stemmed from my inability to grasp why there would be such harsh criticism of, what appears to be, a group of sincere people trying to do a good thing, and my outrage comes from the stark realization that crimes against humanity are still permitted to be perpetrated.

Yes, I said, "permitted." I realize that we're talking about a very complex situation. I realize that crimes against humanity have been committed since the birth of humanity; and I realize that there is no simple solution to stopping the abuse of all sentient beings wherever they live, but I cannot come to terms with why, after eons of human existence on this planet, murder, mutilation, and slavery are allowed to continue.

Are we not, after all, inhabitants of one world? Are we not, after all, interdependent on one another? Are we not, after all, best served through serving others?

I have heard and read the criticisms. I can understand the reasoning of some and reject the reasoning of others.

I am not an expert in geopolitics or world affairs. I can only set out to do the research, to the extent that I am privy to information, and try to make sense of the story. My work is unfinished. I am attempting to build context. What I am offering here is an introduction to the story.

To that end, you will see many quotes, all of which I have endeavored to accurately cite. I have tried to sequence events so as to give the reader a big picture and broad perspective. I encourage you to question my work. Your best chance of truly understanding what's going on here relies on your own ability to critically analyze what you read, see, and hear.

Yes, the events surrounding Joseph Kony and the Lord's Resistance Army are very complex and the solutions to ending the violence are not simple, but I must maintain my simple position that murder, mutilation, and slavery are unacceptable and must be stopped.

You may notice that I have refrained from commenting on the personal lives of any Invisible Children's staff. This is intentional. My story is about stopping Joseph Kony and the LRA. It is not about anything else.

In the end, my intention and firm desire is to contribute to the end of crimes against humanity.

Viral Media and Social Change

"There's something happening here
What it is ain't exactly clear
There's a man with a gun over there
Telling me I got to beware

I think it's time we stop, children, what's that sound?
Everybody look what's going down."

Buffalo Springfield.

There is something happening here – on Earth, right now. In case you haven't gotten out much lately, you need to know there's a viral revolution going on and, with all due respect to Gill Scott Herron, the revolution may not be televised, but it will be texted and tweeted.

The KONY2012 movement is here – now, and may be our next best indication that social change really can be woven into the fabric of humankind by the very weavers of destiny – us.

But… and this is a big But, how long will our collective unconsciousness stick to the moment. How sticky is our stickiness?

Yes, this latest social media phenomenon is phenomenal. By the time you read this, the number of views cited on any particular day (or, for that matter, hour) will be ancient history, but here's the current gist. Within two weeks of its original posting on Vimeo.com, beginning with 20 views per day, the KONY2012 video was at 58,000 views and jumped to 3.5 million views in 3 days. From a Monday through the next Wednesday, the video experienced 1.8 million views on You Tube. Collectively, the video experienced over 7 million views in less than a week. Most of this sharing took place via Facebook and Twitter.

By March 17, 2012, only weeks after its launch, the film had over 80 million views.

Here's the rub. How many major personal, political, and environmental tragedies do you recall deeply enough to act upon? What was the latest news you heard – the latest tragedy you witnessed vicariously? How much can you hold in your head and your heart? Can you identify one person, by name, who suffered unimaginable pain or death?

Note that by April 20, 2012, the KONY2012 Part II video experienced only 1.8 million views ~ a 98% decrease!

Get the picture? Call me crazy, but I call it short term memory syndrome and compassion fatigue. Joseph Kony and the atrocities associated with his name may fall out of our minds immediately after the next horrendous tragedy, but the awareness that the democratic use of social media has wrought will change the game. All of these experiences – "forgotten" or put aside and cast off are being written on our collective conscience.

Can this be true?

According to a study presented by David Langley and Tijs van den Broek of The Netherlands Organization for Applied Scientific Research, presented at the 2010 Internet Politics and Policy Conference, the conclusion is clear.

In their report, "Sustainable Behavior: Case Analysis and Policy Implications," they tell us,

> *"...the use of social media applications by social entrepreneurs and a wide range of organizations to mobilize the masses has begun and firms and government would be well advised to take steps now to understand how these developments will impact upon them. They will need to devise strategies and policies for both reacting to groups which suddenly gain massive support as well as proactively engaging with their target groups by using the emerging strengths of the social media."* [i]

Can we really change the world?

Well, Gandhi told us to, *"Be the change you want to see in the world."* So, perhaps we can.

If we can agree that living like we want the world to change is a viable alternative to apathy and fatalism, we'll need to envision what that change will look like.

If we can agree that being the change we want to see means living in a world where the planet we inhabit is well cared for; and if we can agree that all inhabitants of Earth, present and future, should have an equal shot at peace and prosperity, then we might begin with a working definition of social justice.

The term "social justice" coined by a Jesuit priest (Luigi Taparelli) in 1840 and based on the teachings of Thomas Aquinas (1225-1274) is obviously not a new idea. While some of the tenets of social justice have been adopted by more recent left leaning activists, its secularization is known to have emerged in the late 20th. Century under the influence of the moral and political philosopher, John Rawls.

Accordingly, social justice recognizes the worth and dignity of every human being. While many critics of the idea of social justice claim there can be no objective standard to social justice or, as moral relativists believe, there can be no objective standard to justice in general, the basic premise here is that social justice rests on the principles of social equality and human rights.

Social equality is taken here to mean equal rights under law. Human rights are understood to be "inalienable fundamental rights to which a person is inherently entitled simply because she or he is a human being." [ii]

In a broader discussion of human rights we would drill down into the classification of human rights into the two categories of civil/political rights and economic/social/cultural rights. In a deeper discussion, we would focus on the finer interpretations and criticisms of human rights and the responsibility of sovereign states to enforce those rights but, for now, we're talking about fundamental human rights.

If we cannot agree on the complex nuances and interpretations of human rights, can we agree that, fundamentally, people are entitled to freedom from slavery and torture?

This begs a question – is murder, mutilation, and child slavery "collective environmentally sustainable behavior?"

If it is not, then what's keeping us from stepping up and correcting unsustainable behaviors?

Langley and van den Broek's Sustainable Behavior report states that there are basically two prevailing barriers to achieving what the researchers term, "collective environmentally sustainable behavior". They define the first barrier to collective sustainable behavior as "fatalism", or the belief that any action taken by potential participants in a social action will not have a significant impact on social change.

Regarding this first barrier, the researchers hypothesized that social media can provide evidence to unsure potential participants as well as help committed participants to share information with potential participants.

They call the second barrier "busyness", or the roadblock of turning favorably disposed people into active participants. This real or perceived lack of time and energy inhibits people from translating a concerned attitude into active behavior.

The researchers' second barrier breaking hypothesis is that social media will not only help participants share their experiences, but can stimulate action by reticent potential participants through "reducing the effort required to act."

There are two outcomes to breaking these barriers. First, when the barriers fall, the level of participation rises dramatically and secondly, the level of impact achieved by an initiative often surprises the masses thereby driving them to further action.

After an empirical analysis of 30 social media applications the researchers found a strong connection between the effects of presenting evidence of a group's goals and achievements with the amount of participation gained from potential participants.

Langley and van den Broek's research goes on to show that, "social media can enable a disruptive force that may affect the power balance between market, government, and consumer groups."

What do you suppose might happen if both of these hypotheses are true?

What do you suppose the implications of this changing power balance might be?

Could it be that the KONY2012 movement is the next big thing to come along in social media and the game changing power of people?

Well, let's find out.

"Millions of young people across the world watching a video about Kony's crimes won't end the brutality. But the massive attention generated by Kony's unprecedented global notoriety should be harnessed to transform good intentions into concrete and effective action." (Ida Sawyer) [iii]

Ida Sawyer is an Africa researcher and advocate at Human Rights Watch. This post was originally featured on Congo Siasa.

"Never doubt that a small group of thoughtful, concerned citizens can change the world. Indeed it is the only thing that ever has."

Margaret Mead

Who is Joseph Kony?

Joseph Kony has been called the world's worst criminal. He is most often known for his brutal tactics of abducting children to be soldiers in his army and to serve as "wives" for his officers. He is a member of the Acholi people, an ethnic group of nearly 1.7 million people counted in districts of Uganda as per a 2002 census.

For a personal look at the lives of a few people affected by his "work", view this *pulitzercenter.org* video.

http://pulitzercenter.org/reporting/congo-lra-joseph-kony-voices-stolen-children-soldiers-wives-human-rights.

Kony was born in 1961 in northern Uganda. His father was a member of the Catholic Church and his mother was an Anglican. Kony served as an altar boy prior to dropping out of school and church at around 15 years of age.

According to Peter Eichstaedt, *"First Kill Your Family: Child Soldiers of Uganda and the Lord's Resistance Army"*, Kony apprenticed to a village witch doctor under his older brother James. When James died, Kony is said to have taken over the position of village witch doctor. [iv]

Kony is known as the head of the Lord's Resistance Army (LRA), a guerrilla group whose ideological mission appears to be a mix of Acholi nationalism, Christian fundamentalism, and mysticism. The LRA aims to establish a theocratic state based on Acholi tradition and the Ten Commandments. [v]

Joseph Kony is considered to be a cult leader. He began to be known as a leader in the wake of the powerful premillennialist *Holy Spirit Movement* popularized by Alice Auma (aka Lakwena).

A premillennialist movement is a Christian end-times theology that believes Jesus Christ will literally and physically reside on Earth for the millennial reign at the Second Coming. It is based on a literal interpretation of versus in the last book in the New Testament (Revelation 20:1-6) wherein Jesus returns to Earth and subsequently reigns at the end of the apocalyptic time of tribulation. This is different than other Christian interpretations and eschatology (the study of the end of things). Two of the other interpretations are postmillennialism (the reign of Jesus occurs before the second coming – a Golden Age of Christian ethics) and amillennialism (the second coming is figurative and non-temporal – rejects the theory that Jesus Christ will reign on Earth for 1000 years), but that's another story.

The *Holy Spirit Movement* was a rebel group. Rebel, in this case, referring to people organizing and acting against the ruling powers of the day. Basically, *The Holy Spirit Movement* was the political wing of the *Holy Spirit Mobile Force*, its military wing, whose mission (1986-1987) was to take down the Ugandan government under Yoweri Museveni and its National Resistance Army. [vi]

Alice Auma (1956-2007), said to be Kony's cousin and now deceased, was an Acholi spirit-medium who led the millennial rebellion against Museveni which Kony continued. Her claim to fame was the channeling of a dead Italian army officer known as Lakwena. The combined persona of the channeled spirit of Lakwena and Alice Auma is known as Alice Lakwena. Lakwena means "messenger". Many Acholi believed this messenger to be a manifestation of the Holy Spirit (the third person of the Christian Trinity).

Kony's religious beliefs are no less fantastic. According to a blog post in the Washington Post, Betty Oyela Bigombe recalled that when she met Kony, his *"costumed followers chanted and splashed butter oil and ashes on themselves to ward off bullets and evil spirits."* [vii]

Betty Oyella Bigombe is the current (2011-2012) State Minister for Water Resources in the Uganda Cabinet and an elected Member of Parliament representing the Amuru District Women's Constituency.

According to a BBC profile, Kony is alleged to have said, *"You must also take oil and draw a cross on your chest, your forehead, and each shoulder, and you make a cross in oil on your gun. They say the oil is the power of the Holy Spirit."* [viii]

When pressed to enter negotiations with Museveni, he is quoted by the BBC as saying, *"I will communicate with Museveni through the holy spirits and not through the telephone."* [ix]

The same BBC profile states that, *"Mr Kony himself is thought to have at least 60 wives, as he and his senior commanders take the pick of the girls they capture. He sees himself as a spirit medium. Young abductees who have escaped from the LRA say that Mr. Kony would tell them he got his instructions from the Holy Spirit and would often preach in tongues."* [x]

According to two other sources (Matthew Green, *"The Wizard of the Nile: The Hunt for Africa's Most Wanted"*, and Beatrice Debut Gulu, *"Portrait of Uganda's Rebel Prophet, Painted by Wives"*) Kony believes in polygamy. As of 2007, the sources state, Kony is believed to have 88 wives and 42 children. [xi xii]

And finally, according to the London Times Online, *"I Will Use the Ten Commandments to Liberate Uganda"*, Kony stands firm that he and the Lord's Resistance Army are fighting for the Ten Commandments. He is quoted by *Times Online* as saying,

"Is it bad? It is not against human rights. And that commandment was not given by Joseph. It was not given by the LRA. No, those commandments were given by God." [xiii]

Which brings us to the LRA.

According to records on the International Criminal Court (October 14, 2005) the LRA has been accused of widespread human rights violations including: murder, abduction, mutilation, and forcing children to participate in hostilities; and, according to the Royal African Society (royalafricansociety.org), there have also been reports of cannibalism and child-sex slavery within the group.

Although it has been regarded as a Christian militia, a report funded by the U.S. Embassy in Kampala asserts that, *"... the LRA has no political program or ideology, at least none that the local population has heard or can understand."* [xiv]

According to the Integrated Regional Information Networks (IRIN*), "...the LRA remains one of the least understood rebel movements in the world, and its ideology, as far as it has one, is difficult to understand."* [xv]

IRIN is a humanitarian focused news agency concentrating on regions that are often under-reported or mis-understood. It is a project of the United Nations but holds editorial independence to ensure impartial coverage without necessarily reflecting the views of the UN. The agency is widely used by academics and the humanitarian aid community.

According to *Invisible Children*, a non-profit founded in 2004 to bring awareness to LRA activities and an end to the abduction and abuses of children, the LRA and Joseph Kony employ brutal tactics to,

> *"...force children to kill their parents or siblings with machetes or blunt tools. He (Kony) abducted girls to be sex slaves for his officers. He brainwashed and indoctrinated the children with his lies and manipulated them with his claim of spiritual powers.*
> *At the height of the conflict in Uganda, children "night commuted." That is, every evening they would walk miles from their homes to the city centers. There, hundreds of children would sleep in school houses, churches, or bus depots to avoid abduction by the LRA.*
> *Kony and the LRA abducted more than 30,000 children in northern Uganda."* [xvi]

Finally, according to KONY2012, a project of Invisible Children, *"the LRA is no longer active in northern Uganda (where it originated) but it continues its campaign of violence in Democratic Republic of Congo, Central African Republic, and South Sudan. In its 26-year history, the LRA has abducted more than 30,000 children and displaced at least 2.1 million people."* [xvii]

What's been done to Stop Him?

On July 8 and September 27, 2005, the International Criminal Court (ICC) issued arrest warrants for Kony, his deputy (Vincent Otti), and three commanders in the LRA (Raska Lukwiva, Okot Odhiambo, and Dominic Ongwen). These men were charged with war crimes and crimes against humanity.

As the LRA leadership had stated they would not surrender unless granted immunity from prosecution, there was concern and an indication that there would be no peaceful negotiation to end the insurgency. [xviii]

Vincent Otti, however, contacted the BBC on November 30, 2005 indicating that the LRA would be open to peace talks with the Ugandan government. This was met with a skeptical openness to a peaceful conflict resolution. [xix]

On June 2, 2006, INTERPOL (International Criminal Police Organization) issued Red Notices for five wanted persons. This was done on behalf of the ICC as the ICC has no police of its own.

INTERPOL, founded in 1923, facilitates international police cooperation.

A Red Notice is one of seven levels of INTERPOL notices. Notices are issued to share information among INTERPOL members.

The Red Notice Requests (provisional) arrest of wanted persons, with a view to extradition. An INTERPOL Red Notice is *"the closest instrument to an international arrest warrant in use today."* [xx]

INTERPOL does not have the authority to issue formal arrest warrants. This is the domain of the sovereign member states.

INTERPOL states that it will only issue notices, *"...if it is satisfied that all the conditions for processing the information have been fulfilled. For example, a notice will not be published if it violates Article 3 of the Constitution, which forbids the Organization from undertaking any intervention or activities of a political, military, religious or racial character."* [xxi]

Then, according to a Human Rights Watch 2006 article (Sudan: Regional Government Pays Ugandan Rebels Not to Attack*)*,

> *"The new regional government of Southern Sudan has ignored the International Criminal Court's warrants for the arrest of four top Ugandan rebel leaders, Human Rights Watch said today. The regional government, which acknowledges that the rebel Lord's Resistance Army (LRA) has committed grave abuses, has an obligation to help bring its leaders to justice.*
>
> *On May 2, representatives of the Southern Sudan government met in southern Sudan with LRA leader Joseph Kony and his second-in-command, Vincent Otti, who are subjects of arrest warrants issued by the International Criminal Court. In a digital recording of the meeting made by the Sudanese participants, Dr. Riek Machar Teny Dhurgon, vice-president of the regional government, can be seen handing over bundles of cash to Kony. On the recording, the vice-president is heard cautioning Kony not to use the money for ammunition."* [xxii]

Thus, indicating that the Government of Southern Sudan had ignored ICC arrest warrants. It is believed that the Government of Southern Sudan supplied the LRA with resources as an incentive to keep them from attacking Sudanese citizens.

Since then, two of the five wanted LRA leaders have been killed and one is rumored to have been killed.

Lukwiya was killed in combat with the Uganda Peoples Defense Force (UPDF), the armed forces of Uganda, on August 12, 2006. [xxiii]

Otti was killed in late 2007. [xxiv]

According to the Invisible Children's website, Otti was killed by Kony for betrayal, reportedly for wanting Kony to sign the Juba Cessation of Hostilities agreement.

The Juba Peace Talks, held in Juba, Sudan (now South Sudan) came about in 2006, when the LRA indicated an interest in negotiations. During this time the LRA set up camp in Garamba National Park in northeastern Congo. The talks continued over a period of two years. Kony allegedly sent a delegation to negotiate on his behalf but did not show up – five times – to sign the Final Peace Agreement.

Again, according to Invisible Children's website, it was suspected that, throughout the talks, Kony used the time to rest and regroup. As a gesture of good faith, the LRA was provided with food, clothing, and medicine during the talks; and it is strongly suspected that the LRA used the opportunity to gain strength and stockpile food.

There is also a belief that Kony ordered fighters to attack villages in the Democratic Republic of Congo during the peace talks.

Odhiambo, according to rumor, was killed in April of 2008.

"The deputy leader of Uganda's rebel Lord's Resistance Army leader has been killed, according to those involved in peace talks. LRA insiders said Okot Odhiambo and eight others were killed as rebels clashed over the proposed deal."
xxv

As far as it is known, only Kony and Ongwen remain at large.

Once the Juba Peace Talks began, the LRA left Uganda and since 2008 have carried out attacks in the border regions of northeastern Congo, South Sudan, and the Central African Republic.

When it became clear that Joseph Kony was not going to sign a peace agreement, a coordinated effort of Uganda, the Democratic Republic of Congo, the Central African Republic, and Sudan, with logistical support and intelligence from the United States, launched Operation Lightning and Thunder to attack the LRA.

Kony learned of the attack and was able to escape.

In retribution for Operation Lightning and Thunder, Ongwen led LRA attacks on villages in the Democratic Republic of Congo beginning on December 24th, 2008. Over the course of two weeks, the LRA killed 865 civilians and abducted 160 more. The mission was reportedly conducted to target churches where families would be gathered for Christmas Eve services.

A year later, the LRA repeated the Christmas massacres in the northeastern Congo area of Makombo as a reminder of its power. Over a period of 5 days (December 14-18, 2009) the LRA killed 321 people and abducted 250 more.

The outside world knew little or nothing of these Makombo massacres. Finally, 3 months later, on March 28, 2009, Human Rights Watch broke the story.

In the United States, President Barack Obama signed the "Lord's Resistance Army Disarmament and Northern Uganda Recovery Act" into law in May of 2010. This bill passed unanimously in both the U.S Senate and the House of Representatives. In total, the bill had 65 senators and 202 representatives as cosponsors.

Essentially, the law intends to,

> *"...stop the LRA, by mandating President Obama to devise an interagency strategy to prevent LRA violence, which should include a multilateral plan to apprehend top LRA leaders, encourage defections of rebel commanders, demobilize child soldiers, and protect civilians from rebel attacks; and invest in sustainable peace, by targeting US assistance to recovery and reconciliation efforts in northern Uganda, which are essential to rebuilding and healing war-affected communities and preventing future conflicts."* [xxvi]

On October 14, 2011, President Obama ordered a deployment of 100 U.S. military advisors (many of whom are from the Army Special Forces) to help combat the LRA. The advisors have a mandate to train, assist, and provided intelligence. While they are armed, they *"will not, themselves, engage LRA forces unless necessary for self-defense."* [xxvii]

President Obama did not need explicit congressional approval to deploy troops as the *Lord's Resistance Army Disarmament and Northern Uganda Recovery Act* authorized, *"increased, comprehensive U.S. efforts to help mitigate and eliminate the threat posed by the LRA to civilians and regional stability."* [xxviii]

On December 14, 2010, Foreign Policy, a magazine division of Washington Post Company, posted the following as part of their *WikiFailed States* issue. Intending to highlight what WikiLeaks cables had to say about lesser known struggles around the globe, the magazine reported,

> *"Sudan's neighbor, Uganda, blames Khartoum for paying and harboring Ugandan rebel Joseph Kony, leader of the Lord's Resistance Army (LRA), a brutal rebel group that has waged the longest-running insurgency in Africa. Ugandan President Yoweri Museveni told U.S. Assistant Secretary of State for African Affairs Jendayi Frazer in September 2007 that 'Sudan, Sudan, Sudan, Sudan' was behind the rebellion's longevity. '[Museveni] said that even if the Khartoum Government could not supply the LRA at previous levels, he believed it was in constant touch with the LRA and smuggling supplies."* [xxix]

This brings us to *Invisible Children* and the *KONY2012* movement.

Invisible Children – The Backstory

Founded in 2004, *Invisible Children, Inc.*, a not-for-profit organization, was established to bring awareness to the LRA and the activities of Joseph Kony. The organization's specific purpose is to put an end to the abductions and abuse of children via the acts of Joseph Kony and the LRA. Invisible Children urges the United States to take a form of military action in central Africa.

The form of military action is not support for additional U.S. troops on the ground. Rather, it is a push for support in information technology and intelligence to stop the LRA.

The group solicits donations, sells merchandise, and distributes videos on the Internet. It also presents its case in high schools and colleges around the United States.

Throughout its history, Invisible Children has won many awards and established a number or programs.

The group's awards include the following:

2007 - Progressive Source Award, TRI podcast for Best Fundraising   .

2008 - Human Security Award.
People's Voice Webby Award.
American Advertising Federation Award.
The Summit Awards, Creative Award category, for Schools for Schools and Displace Me websites.

2009 – Interactive Media Awards, Rescue website.

2010 - 2011 - Stay Classy Award, Most Effective Awareness Campaign.

2011 - The LRA Crisis Tracker for Best in Show 2011 MediaPost Creative Media Awards.

The Invisible Children organization employs 43 full-time staff in the U.S. and 100 in Uganda. They are currently expanding permanent staff into the conflict areas of Congo and the Central African Republic.

Beginning in 2005 in Uganda, the group worked with local leadership to develop its programs. Local visionary leadership helped form Invisible Children Uganda (ICU), who works with approximately 100 Ugandan professionals and four international staff members managing program activities and communicating with Invisible Children and international supporters.

The following Programs established by Invisible Children are explained on their website.

Invisible Children programs in northern Uganda

The Lord's Resistance Army was active in northern Uganda for more than two decades. It has left Uganda, but the region will be in recovery for years to come. Since 2005, Invisible Children has been focused on providing access to quality education and improving the livelihood of a post-conflict community.

Legacy Scholarship Program
"Provides merit-based scholarships and mentoring to motivated and talented secondary and university students from northern Uganda who were affected by the conflict. Currently supporting 590 secondary students and 250 university students, the program is educating the next generation of leaders in northern Uganda."

Schools for Schools
"Partnering with 11 of the top secondary schools in northern Uganda affected by the LRA insurgency, Schools for Schools works to construct and renovate school structures while also building teacher capacity and developing curriculum."

Mend
"A social enterprise geared toward facilitating financial independence and development for women formerly abducted by the LRA. The program currently supports 16 seamstresses who use their tailoring skills to create unique, high-quality handbags. Each Mend product carries the name of the seamstress who made it and seams a personal connection between the products, their makers, and consumers."

Invisible Children Campaigns

Invisible Children has also initiated a number of campaigns prior to KONY2012.

According to its website,

"The Invisible Children movement is a core part of our mission. It is a global community of young people that galvanizes international support to bring a permanent end to LRA violence through mass awareness campaigns and strategic advocacy efforts. By focusing on a single objective, we've rallied millions of people behind the idea that human life is equal and that where you live shouldn't determine whether you live."

The Movement page of the site also introduces "The Fourth Estate", a conference for movement participants and international justice experts.

THE FOURTH ESTATE

"The movement is built on the shoulders of courageous young people, but its strength lies in a commitment to collaboration. In August of 2011, Invisible Children supporters from all over the world came together in San Diego for a conference called The Fourth Estate. Participants interacted with experts in the field of international justice and discussed their role in global humanitarian efforts."

Again, from the website,

Past Campaigns

"Unlike any other initiative at Invisible Children, our big events have a way of bringing it all together. They simultaneously appeal to our government, educate our supporters, and bring together a group of people dedicated to making a difference. Through power in numbers and strength in community, we shed light on situations that merit attention and inspire action that changes culture, policy, and lives. Take a moment to view our past campaign videos and see how young people around the world have rallied together to use their voice for change."

Global Night Commute – 2006

In April of 2006, the *Global Night Commute* (GNC) campaign took place to bring attention to the plight of children from 3 to 17 years old from Acholiland in northern Uganda. Referred to as "night commuters", the children walked up to 12 miles each night from *internally displaced person* camps to towns nearby to escape capture by the LRA.

Beginning in 1996, the Ugandan government required *internally displaced people* to enter government run camps supposedly for their safety. The camps were rife with disease and violence. Apparently, they were not safe from LRA violence. At one point in the conflict, approximately 1.7 million people lived in these camps throughout the region. An entire generation of Acholi people were born and raised in these camps.

During the GNC campaign, youths from around the world, to show support for Ugandan children, walked to city centers and spent the night in parks. The effort took place in 130 cities in seven countries. Over 80,000 people participated in the campaign.

In an effort to facilitate change in U.S. policies regarding Africa's longest running war, the slogan for the event was, "On April 29th. We gathered. To make a difference. To end a war."

Displace Me – 2007

Displace Me took place on April 28, 2007 in 15 cities. It was attended by 68,000 people with the intention of bringing awareness to *displacement camps* in northern Uganda. Displacement Camps are temporary facilities for people coerced into forced migration.

The stated goals of the campaign were to:

> *"... educate participants about displacement camps in the North by simulating, as best as possible, the experience of living in an IDP camp."*

> *"... create greater national and international attention of the humanitarian crises in northern Uganda."*

> *"... garner the political attention needed to see a peaceful resolution to the war in northern Uganda, primarily through the appointment of one senior level U.S. diplomat."*

Participants in the *Displace Me* campaign built "huts" out of cardboard boxes. They were rationed food and water throughout the night, and heard video testimonies from people living in IDP camps.

First Lady, at the time, Laura Bush directly addressed the participants via a prerecorded video speech. The event was concluded with participants writing letters to their government leaders and the President of Uganda.

The campaign featured 21 minutes of silence recognizing 21 years of war in the regions at the time.

The Rescue – 2009

Simple words cannot express the message in this video. You simply must view it to appreciate it. Please ~ navigate to You Tube and watch it here,

http://www.youtube.com/watch?v=aUj2Ypa7cYc

LRA Crisis Tracker

Another facet of the Invisible Children organization is the *LRA Crisis Tracker*, a real time attack tracker of the LRA conflict.

You can link to it at, http://www.lracrisistracker.com/.

The LRA Crisis Tracker is a data collection system and real-time mapping platform. The system was created to bring, *"an unprecedented level of transparency to the atrocities of the Lord's Resistance Army."* (Invisible Children's website).

Information is sourced from Invisible Children's Early Warning Radio Network, local NGO's, and UN agencies. The tool, jointly developed by Invisible Children, Resolve, and Digitaria, is meant to help governments, policy makers, and humanitarian organizations respond to the conflict.

The Early Warning Radio Network links remote locations to a central hub that connects to the LRA Crisis Tracker, thereby alerting the world to what may have been unseen atrocities committed by the LRA.

According to a *Pulitzer Center on Crisis Reporting* blog post,

> *"The HF radios will establish long-distance communication between remote locations and act as an early warning mechanism for towns and villages in surrounding areas. In an aim to help prevent the future movements of the LRA, communities can use the solar-powered radios to notify and contact security forces of LRA sightings and attacks. The HF radio's notification and response system aim to prevent the LRA from fluid, undeterred movements -- and to make future atrocities like the Christmas Massacres less likely."* [xxx]

Resolve (theresolve.org) is, a Washington D.C.-based NGO advocating to the U.S. and international policy makers for an end to atrocities being perpetrated by the Lord's Resistance Army.

KONY 2012 – The Movement

The KONY2012 movement is intended to "Stop Kony". The plan is to have him arrested by making him famous.

The "Stop Kony" message is embodied in the KONY2012 video which describes the tactics of Joseph Kony and the LRA.

You can view it at,

http://www.youtube.com/watch?v=Y4MnpzG5Sqc.

In the film, Jacob, a young African boy, tells us about the death of his brother and gives us a glimpse of what life is like for children threatened by the LRA and Kony's rule.

Jason Russell, director and co-founder of Invisible Children, promises Jacob that he will help stop Kony. The video is enhanced by the responses of Russell's young son to the plight and sufferings of the children in Jacob's world.

According to the KONY2012 Website the goal of the movement is as follows.

"Invisible Children has been working for 9 years to end Africa's longest-running armed conflict. U.S. military advisers are currently deployed in Central Africa on a "time-limited" mission to stop Kony and disarm the LRA. If Kony isn't captured this year, the window will be gone."

This is an important point. The military advisers deployed by President Obama have a very short window to accomplish their mission. Magnifying public awareness of the situation may well help the cause. The viral explosion of the video coupled with the attention getting strategies of employing popular and political game changers may help to mitigate the barriers to action noted earlier.

The KONY2012 action plan is designed to help ensure two outcomes.

1) That Joseph Kony is known as the World's Worst War Criminal.

2) That U.S. and international efforts to stop Kony are bolstered with a more comprehensive strategy for disarmament, demobilization, and reintergration (DDR).

This is an integral part of the organization's stated goals. Increased public awareness and action may well encourage lawmakers and the military to come up with *"...a more comprehensive strategy for disarmament, demobilization, and reintegration."*

Here's how making Joseph Kony famous can help the cause. From the KONY2012 website,

> *"Invisible Children's KONY 2012 campaign aims to make Joseph Kony famous, not to celebrate him, but to raise support for his arrest and set a precedent for international justice. In this case, notoriety translates to public support. If people know about the crimes that Kony has been committing for 26 years, they will unite to stop him.*
>
> *Secondly, we want Kony to be famous so that when he is stopped, he will be a visible, concrete example of international justice. Then other war criminals will know that their mass atrocities will not go unnoticed or unpunished."*

This, too, is a very important point. The viral nature of people rising up for justice can spread across the globe. There are some very powerful key ideas in this statement.

"...set a precedent for international justice." and, *"...a visible, concrete example of international justice."*

Think about that. Imagine a global precedent for international justice. Imagine international justice.

We're seeing glimpses of this, of course, with the recent arrival of the Arab Spring.

Since December of 2010, rulers have been disposed in Tunisia, Egypt, Libya, and Yemen. Civil uprisings have erupted in Bahrain and Syria, while major protests have broken out in Algeria, Iraq, Jordan, Kuwait, Morocco, and Oman. Along with this, there have been minor protests in Lebanon, Mauritania, Saudi Arabia, Sudan, and Western Sahara.

All of these uprisings have two things in common – social media and civil resistance. Together, awareness, organization, and communication appear to be the saving grace of the day. The battle is on. The jury may be out, but the evidence is piling up. Social media and civil resistance are a one-two punch.

Clearly, the situation in central Africa is somewhat different than in the Middle East. The isolated nature of the geopolitical landscape coupled with the "powerlessness" of the people may call for different approaches, but the concept is the same – awareness, organization, and communication (attitude, alignment, action) – takes the day.

When you combine awareness, organization, and communication with affecting our culture's shape shifters and the people with the power to change policy, you have a chance to change the world.

When you visit the KONY2012.com website, you'll see photos of twenty "Culturemakers" and twelve "Policymakers".

For the "Culturemakers", the site says, "When they speak, the world listens."

For the "Policymakers", the site says, "When they agree, change happens."

You can easily click on the images and send each one a message.

The list of "Culturemakers" includes:

-TV Personality/Entrepreneur	Oprah
-Entrepreneur	Mark Zuckerberg
-Singer	Lady Gaga
-Actress/Humanitarian	Angelina Jolie
-Actor/Humanitarian	George Clooney
-TV Personality	Bill O'Reilly
-Entrepreneur	Bill Gates
-Rapper	Jay-Z
-Singer	Justin Bieber
-Minister	Rick Warren
-TV Personality	Ellen DeGeneres
-Actor/Humanitarian	Ben Affleck
-Singer	Rihanna
-TV Host	Stephen Colbert
-Investor/Philanthropist	Warren Buffett
-Singer/Songwriter	Taylor Swift
-TV/Radio Personality	Ryan Seacrest
-Athlete	Tim Tebow
-Radio Personality	Rush Limbaugh
-Singer/Humanitarian	Bono

The list of "Policymakers" includes:

-Former U.S. President	George W. Bush
-Former Secretary of State	Condoleezza Rice
-Senator (D-MA)	John Kerry
-Former U.S. President	Bill Clinton
-Senator (D-NV)	Harry Reid
-Congressman (R-OH)	John Boehner
-Congresswoman (R-TX)	Kay Granger
-Presidential Candidate (R)	Mitt Romney
-Canadian Prime Minister	Stephen Harper
-UN Secretary General	Ban Ki-Moon
-Congresswoman (R-FL)	Lleana Ros-Lehtinen
-Senator (D-VT)	Patrick Leahy

While on the KONY2012 website, you can take the simple action steps of buying or downloading the action kit, pledging your support, and donating to the campaign. While these may seem to be rather innocuous ways to contribute to the campaign, the net effect of millions of relatively tiny voices creates a synergy that will make a difference.

Criticisms of Invisible Children and KONY2012

While there have been hundreds of thousands of comments in support of Invisible Children and the KONY2012 campaign, the criticisms and challenges to the organization's efforts have been less than kind and, in some cases, fierce.

In response to the adversarial nature of the criticisms, the organization has attempted to address the critiques on its Invisible Children site.

In an attempt to provide, *"...a source for accurate information about Invisible Children's mission, financials and approach to stopping LRA violence"*, the group begins by clearly restating its mission in the form of an official response.

> *"Invisible Children's mission is to stop LRA violence and support the war-affected communities in East and Central Africa. These are the three ways we achieve this mission; each is essential:*
>
> *1) Make the world aware of the LRA. This includes making documentary films and touring them around the world so that they are seen for free by millions of people.*
>
> *2) Channel energy from viewers of IC films into large-scale advocacy campaigns to stop the LRA and protect civilians.*
>
> *3) Operate programs on the ground in LRA-affected areas that provide protection, rehabilitation and development assistance."*

The organization states that they spend one third of their funds on each of the three goals of: documenting human rights abuses, engaging in advocacy and awareness campaigns, and working with on-the-ground rehabilitation and development projects.

The group states that it is 100% committed to financial transparency and to communicating its mission in plain language. This, they say, allows people to make an informed decision about supporting the organization's efforts.

Regarding financials, Invisible Children's financial statements for the previous 5 years are publically posted online at: http://www.invisiblechildren.com/financials.html.

Invisible Children Inc., states that, for the Fiscal Year 2011, they spent 80.46% on programs to further the three-fold mission; 16.24% on administration and management costs; and 3.22% on direct fundraising.

Charity Navigator (http://www.charitynavigator.org/), an independent charity evaluator, gives Invisible Children 3 out of 4 stars as an Overall Rating and 4 stars on its Financial Rating. Four Stars is the highest rating available. [xxxi]

The group received 2 stars on Accountability and Transparency because it does not yet have 5 independent voting members on the board of directors.

There are currently 4 board members and the organization is in the process of interviewing for a 5th. in order to regain its 4-star rating by 2013.

Invisible Children is independently audited by Considine and Considine, Certified Public Accountants. The organization is audited each year and is currently in full compliance with their 501(c)3 nonprofit status.

According to the Invisible Children website,

"...all of our audits have resulted in unqualified opinions on the audit reports. An unqualified opinion means that the auditors believe the financial statements are free of material misstatement and are in conformity with generally accepted accounting principles of the United States."

Charity Navigator states, regarding its Accountability and Transparency Performance Metrics that, for Invisible Children,

"The charity's audited financials were prepared by an independent accountant, but it did not have an audit oversight committee. In this case, we deduct 7 points from the charity's Accountability and Transparency score."

Regarding Donor Privacy Policy, Charity Navigator notes that, for Invisible Children,

> *"The charity has a written privacy policy published on its website which enables donors to tell the charity to remove their names and contact information from mailing lists the charity sells, trades or shares. Opt-out requirements vary from one charity to the next, but all require donors to take some action to protect their privacy. In these cases, we deduct 3 points from the charity's Accountability and Transparency score."*

The Donor Privacy Policy regarding the use of personal information by charities to telemarket and distribute "junk mail" is rated according to whether the charity has a written privacy policy (no selling or trading names), an opt out provision, or no policy. Invisible Children has an opt out provision.

In terms of criticisms relating to the group's lobbying efforts, Invisible Children responds by stating that they lobby all members of Congress, regardless of party affiliation and that they do not endorse a political party. As a charity, they are encouraged by Federal laws to lobby within specified limits. These limits are ensured by the filing an additional Schedule with Form 990, providing financial details surrounding their involvement in lobbying.

Having elected 501(h) status is part of their commitment to voluntarily report lobbying expenditures to the IRS.

Regarding the strategy to arrest Kony, the KONY2012 campaign refers to Kony's refusal to negotiate an end to the violence and his strategy of using peace talks to build his army's strength through targeted abduction campaigns. The campaign notes that Kony is not being brought to justice, in part, because regional African governments are *"...often not adequately committed to the task,"* and *"...because they lack some of the specific capabilities that would help them do so."*

The campaign is calling on U.S. leadership to address both problems. It supports U.S. deployment of advisers, the provision of intelligence, increased diplomacy to hold regional governments accountable to protecting civilians, and advocates for broader measures to assist communities being affected by LRA attacks. Specifically, KONY2012 seeks increased funding for programs aimed at helping abductees escape and return to their homes and families.

The Council on Foreign Relations (C.F.R.) has charged groups like Invisible Children with *"...manipulat[ing] facts for strategic purposes, exaggerating the scale of LRA abductions and murders."* [xxxii]

In response, Resolve, a partner organization with Invisible Children, called the accusation a, *"...serious charge...published with no accompanying substantiation."* [xxxiii]

Along with this, Invisible Children has asserted that the numbers of child abductions the charity uses, *"...are often the same numbers as ones used by Human Rights Watch and the United Nations."*

The same C.F.R. article stated that organizations such as Invisible Children, *"...rarely refer to the Ugandan atrocities or those of Sudan's People's Liberation Army."*

Regarding the Ugandan human rights record, Invisible Children has stated that it does not defend any human rights abuses committed by the Ugandan government or the Ugandan army (UPDF), nor does it channel any of its money to the Ugandan government or any other government. It calls, instead, for coordinated efforts among regional governments.

Criticism has come from Uganda as well.

Rosbell Kagumire, a Ugandan journalist specializing in peace and conflict reporting, noted that the KONY2012 movement, *"...paints a picture of Uganda six or seven years ago, that is totally not how it is today. It's highly irresponsible."* [xxxiv]

At a showing of the film in the northern Uganda town of Lira in March 2012, some of the approximately 35,000 attendees jeered. Some threw rocks at the screen and at the group (The African Youth Initiative Network) showing the film. The complaint was that the film was more focused on the filmmakers and Kony rather than the conflict's victims and was, *"...more about whites than Ugandans."* [xxxv]

When The Daily Telegraph interviewed residents in the former rebel center of Gulu, Uganda, the director of the community health organization, Dr. Beatrice Mpora said,

"What that video says is totally wrong, and it can cause us more problems than help us (...) There has not been a single soul from the LRA here since 2006. Now we have peace, people are back in their homes, they are planting their fields, they are starting their businesses. That is what people should help us with." [xxxvi]

The African Youth Initiative Network intends to continue showing the film, but with more context given prior to screening. This, they hope, will help African viewers understand the message more clearly.

Regarding *"... painting a picture of Uganda six or seven years ago...."* and exaggerating the current impact of LRA activities, Invisible Children responds that,

"Since the LRA left Uganda in 2006, Invisible Children has been publicly denouncing their atrocities in DR Congo, South Sudan, and the Central African Republic (CAR), while continuing to work with now-peaceful communities in post-conflict northern Uganda."

Invisible Children also refers to its LRA Crisis Tracker and Early Warning Radio Network as tools to provide concrete data to help dispel unfounded rumors regarding LRA attacks. The systems rate each reported incident on a scale of 1 to 5 as to whether the event has actually occurred and whether it was committed by the LRA.

Regarding oversimplification of a complex issue, Invisible Children admits that many nuances of a 26-year conflict are lost or overlooked in the film, but states that it is an entry point to the conflict, and that the organization provides several ways for supporters to learn more.

The group strives to garner wide public support and has sought to explain the conflict in an easily understandable format. The film focuses on the core attributes of LRA leadership and its infringement on the most basic of human rights. It clearly displays, *"...the image of a madman who manipulates children spiritually for his own tactical gains."*

Regarding perpetuating the 'White Man's Burden' and the 'Savior Complex', the group points out that its programs are, *"...implemented with continuous input from, and in respect of the knowledge and experience of, local communities and their leaders."*

Invisible Children recognizes that local solutions are needed to fill critical humanitarian gaps. They state that 95% of IC's leadership and staff on the ground are Ugandans.

Regarding the photo of Invisible Children founders with guns, the group states that it was an irresponsible "joke photo". Jason Russell, co-founder of Invisible Children, in his statement about the photo says,

> *"The ironic thing about this photo is that I HATE guns. I always have. Back in 2008 I wanted this war to end, like we all did, peacefully, through peace talks. But Kony was not interested in that; he kept killing. And we still don't want war. We don't want him killed and we don't want bombs dropped. We want him alive and captured and brought to justice."*

Finally, in a personal note on the Invisible Children website, the organization states,

> *"We've done our utmost to be as inclusive, transparent, and factual as possible. We built this organization with "seeing is believing" in mind, and that's why we are a media-based organization. We WANT you to see everything we are doing, because we are proud of it. Though we would no longer consider ourselves naive, we have always sought counsel from those who know much more. We have never claimed a desire to "save Africa," but, instead, an intent to inspire Western youth to "do more than just watch." And in Central Africa, focus on locally-led long-term development programs that enable children to take responsibility for their own futures and the futures of their countries. Our programs are carefully researched and developed initiatives by incredible members of the local community that address the need for quality education, mentorship, the redevelopment of schools, resettlement from IDP camps, and rehabilitation from war. If you know anyone who has been there to see it first hand, there is no doubt they will concur. Also, we have invited you to join us on www.LRACrisisTracker.com, which we established as a way to bring you near real-time reports from the ground, making available to the public the same information received by humanitarians working on the ground.*
>
> *But, credibility in the eyes of policymakers, fellow non-profit workers, LRA-affected communities, and YOU is our most important asset, so we would like to encourage you, if you have critiques, to get specific: find facts, dig deeper, and we'll gladly continue the conversation from there. If encountering something you disagree with, suggest an alternative to what we are doing- and we will absolutely take heed. If it's a matter of opinion, taste, humor, or style: we apologize, and will have to agree to disagree. As the poet Ke$ha (ed. That's how it's spelled) says, "we are who we are."*
>
> *Let's focus on what matters, and what we DO agree on: Joseph Kony needs to be stopped. And when that happens, peace is the limit. This is the beautiful beginning of an ending that is just the beginning. We are defending tomorrow. And it's hopeful."*

Next?

Whether you are a supporter or detractor, one thing is clear. We need to focus on what matters to the people of central Africa still living in the shadow of the next LRA attack.

Yes, the LRA is no longer in Uganda. And, yes, we've been told there have been fewer attacks than before, but the attacks continue in neighbouring countries. No attack is acceptable.

Kony's instant, viral notoriety can help nudge shape-shifters and game-changers into action. Policy makers hold the keys, but people are the makers of those keys. Whether or not there is a direct threat to American security is not at issue. Whether all people, simply because they inhabit the same planet, have the right to safety and freedom from harm at the hands of other human beings is the issue. We're talking about the fundamental right to life.

Citizen activism and social media will continue to contribute to the cause. The sheer numbers of people stepping away from the twin barriers of fatalism and busyness will have a profound effect on the consciousness of people around the globe.

Capturing and bringing Joseph Kony to justice is crucially important. He is a real-live visual manifestation of a human rights violator. His capture would weaken the position of the LRA and send a message to the world. Behaviour such as his and that of his army is unsustainable and unacceptable. If you commit a crime against humanity, you will be stopped – period.

Simply capturing Kony is not enough. The LRA threat and others like it will continue; but there's no room for fatalism here. The arrests of human rights violating central figures, wherever they surface, will open opportunities to demobilize forces, rescue abducted children, stop abuses, and help end future attacks.

A complex situation? You bet, but that does not mean there shouldn't be accountability for serious crimes against humanity.

During the efforts to capture Kony, and after he is captured, civilians will need to be protected from retaliatory attacks. On the ground intelligence and communication systems must be operational, protected, and maintained. Defection from the LRA needs to be encouraged. Defectors and released captives will need rehabilitation and treatment. Existing humanitarian projects must continue to be supported.

Activists and workers from many organizations need to be involved. Regional governments need to cooperate across borders. Governments, militaries, peace keepers, social activists, religious leaders, aid organizations, and defenders of human rights must forego polar and paralysing, idle differences. We must come together for one purpose – LIFE.

Sound idealistic?

It is.

It's an ideal whose time has come.

Find your place. Find your pace. Find your peace.

Take action.

> **"Be the change you want to see in the world."**
> *Mahatma Gandhi*

Biography

Tim O'Connor is a writer, teacher, and bookseller. He has lived and worked in Vermont for 28 years, concentrating on raising a family, building a home, growing food, and practicing Yoga. His interests run wide and deep, but are primarily centered on issues regarding human rights, environmental stewardship, and the impact of globalization on local economies. To that end, Tim researches and writes on a variety of topics intended to contribute to a sustainable future for humankind.

Endnotes

[i] David Langley and Tijs van den Broek, *"Sustainable Behavior: Case Analysis and Policy Implications"*, The Netherlands Organization for Applied Scientific Research, 2010.

[ii] Sepúlveda, Magdalenas, et.al, *"Human Rights Reference Handbook"* (3rd ed.), Ciudad Colon, Costa Rica: University of Peace, 2004.

[iii] Ida Sawyer, *"Special to the Pulitzer Center"*, March 14, 2012.

[iv] Peter Eichstaedt, *"First Kill Your Family: Child Soldiers of Uganda and the Lord's Resistance Army"*, Lawrence Hill Books, 2009.

[v] Ruddy Doom and Koen Vlassenroot, *"Kony's Message: A New Kone? The Lord's Resistance Army in Northern Uganda"*, Oxford Journals/Royal African Society, 1999.

[vi] Tim Allen, *"Understanding Alice: Uganda's Holy Spirit Movement in Context"*, Journal of the International African Institute, Vol. 61, No. 3, Diviners, Seers and Prophets in Eastern Africa.

[vii] Nora Boustany, *"The Woman Behind Uganda's Peace Hopes"*, Washington Post blog, July 11, 2007.

[viii] BBC News. October 7, 2005.

[ix] Ibid.

[x] Ibid.

[xi] Matthew Green, *"The Wizard of the Nile: The Hunt for Africa's Most Wanted"*, Portobello Books, 2008.

[xii] Beatrice Debut Gulu, *"Portrait of Uganda's Rebel Prophet, Painted by Wives"*, Mail & Guardian Online, February 10, 2006.

xiii London Times Online, *"I Will Use the Ten Commandments to Liberate Uganda"*.

xiv Robert Gersony, *"Results of a Field-Based Assessment of the Civil Conflicts in Northern Uganda"* (PDF). *"The Anguish of Northern Uganda"*. Kampala, Uganda: USAID.

xv IRIN: *UGAND-SUDAN: "Ri-Kwangba: Meeting Point"*, June 2, 2007.

xvi http://www.invisiblechildren.com/

xvii http://www.kony2012.com/

xviii BBC, *"Court Moves against Uganda Rebels"*, October 7 2005.

xix Ibid. *"Ugandans Welcome Rebel Overture"*, November 30, 2005
.
xx

http://www.justice.gov/usao/eousa/foia_reading_room/usam/title9/crm00611.htm.

xxi *Interpol factsheet* PDF.

xxii Human Rights Watch, *"Sudan: Regional Government Pays Ugandan Rebels Not to Attack"*, June 3, 2006.

xxiii International Criminal Court, *"Statement by the Chief Prosecutor Luis Moreno Ocampo on the Confirmation of the Death of Raska Lukwiya"* PDF, November 7, 2006.

xxiv BBC News, *"Uganda's LRA Confirm Otti Death"*, January 23, 2008.

xxv IBID. *"Ugandan LRA Rebel Deputy 'Killed'"*, April 14, 2008.

xxvi THERESOLVE.ORG.

xxvii New York Times, *"Obama Sending 100 Armed Advisers to Africa to Help Fight Renegade Group"*, October 14, 2011.

[xxviii] Ibid.

[xxix] Foreign Policy, Washington Post Company, *"WikiFailed States"*, December 14, 2010.

[xxx] Pulitzer Center on Crisis Reporting, *"A New Chapter: Early Warning Radio Network"*, Meghan Moore, April 12, 2011.

[xxxi] Charity Navigator, *"Evaluation of Invisible Children, Inc."*. http://www.charitynavigator.org/index.cfm?bay=search.summary&orgid=12429

[xxxii] foreignaffairs.com,Schomerus Mareike, et.al.*"Obama Takes on the LRA: Why Washington Sent Troops to Central Africa"*.

[xxxiii] theresolve.org., **"Resolve Responds to Recent Foreign Affairs Article"**, November 17, 2011.

[xxxiv] YouTube, *"My Response to KONY2012"*, Rosbell Kagumire
.

[xxxv] Wall Street Journal, *"Kony Screening Inflames Ugandans"*, Nicholas Bariyo; Erica Orden March 16, 2012.

[xxxvi] The Telegraph, *"Joseph Kony 2012: Growing Outrage in Uganda over Film"*, Mike Pflanz, March 8,2012.